A Brief History of the U.S. Army in World War II

CENTER OF MILITARY HISTORY
UNITED STATES ARMY
WASHINGTON, D.C., 1992

Introduction

World War II was the largest and most violent armed conflict in the history of mankind. However, the half century that now separates us from that conflict has exacted its toll on our collective knowledge. While World War II continues to absorb the interest of military scholars and historians, as well as its veterans, a generation of Americans has grown to maturity largely unaware of the political, social, and military implications of a war that, more than any other, united us as a people with a common purpose.

Highly relevant today, World War II has much to teach us, not only about the profession of arms, but also about military preparedness, global strategy, and combined operations in the coalition war against fascism. During the next several years, the U.S. Army will participate in the nation's 50th anniversary commemoration of World War II. The commemoration will include the publication of various materials to help educate Americans about that war. The works produced will provide great opportunities to learn about and renew pride in an Army that fought so magnificently in what has been called "the mighty endeavor."

A Brief History of the U.S. Army in World War II highlights the major ground force campaigns during the six years of the war, offers suggestions for further reading, and provides Americans an opportunity to learn about the Army's role in World War II. This brochure was prepared at the U.S. Army Center of Military History by Wayne M. Dzwonchyk (Europe) and John Ray Skates (Pacific). I hope this absorbing account of that period will enhance your appreciation of American achievements during World War II.

M. P. W. Stone
Secretary of the Army

Contents

The War in Europe 3
    The Outbreak of War 4
    The United States Enters the War................. 8
    The North African Campaign 10
    Sicily and Italy................................ 15
    The Cross-Channel Attack 17
    Battles of Attrition 21
    The Battle of the Bulge......................... 22
    The Final Offensive............................ 23

The Pacific War.............................. 29
    Japan on the Offensive 31
    The Tide Turns 34
    Twin Drives to American Victory 39
    Aftermath 43

Maps

Allied Operations in World War II, 1942–1945 12
The Pacific and Adjacent Theaters, 1942–1945 36

Further Readings 45

"OMAHA Beach" by Gary Sheahan. This was the one sector of the Normandy coast where the German defenses had begun to reach the expectations of Field Marshal Rommel, and here the Allied invasion of France faced its greatest crisis. (Army Art Collection)

The War in Europe

The War in Europe

World War I left unresolved the question of who would dominate Europe. The tremendous dislocations caused by the war laid the groundwork for the collapse of democratic institutions there and set the stage for a second German attempt at conquest. A worldwide depression that began in 1929 destroyed the fragile democratic regime in Germany. In 1933 Adolf Hitler led to power the National Socialist German Workers' (Nazi) Party, a mass movement that was virulently nationalistic, antidemocratic, and anti-Semitic. He ended parliamentary government, assumed dictatorial powers, and proclaimed the Third Reich. The Nazi government increased the strength of the German armed forces and sought to overturn the Versailles Treaty, to recover German territory lost at the peace settlement, and to return to the so-called Fatherland German-speaking minorities within the borders of surrounding countries.

The ultimate goal of Hitler's policy was to secure "living space" for the German "master race" in eastern Europe. A gambler by instinct, Hitler relied on diplomatic bluff and military innovation to overcome Germany's weaknesses. He played skillfully on the divisions among the European powers to gain many of his aims without war. With the Italian Fascist dictator Benito Mussolini he announced a Rome-Berlin alliance (the Axis) in 1935. Meanwhile, in the Far East, the Japanese—the only Asian industrial power—coveted the natural resources of China and Southeast Asia, but found their expansion blocked by European colonial powers or by the United States. Having seized Manchuria in 1931, they began a war against China in 1937. The League of Nations failed to counter effectively Japanese aggression in Manchuria and an Italian invasion of Ethiopia. Soon Germany, Italy, and Japan became allies, facing Western democratic governments that wanted to avoid another war and the Soviet Union whose Communist government was widely distrusted.

The people of the United States, having rejected the Versailles Treaty and the Covenant of the League of Nations after World War I, remained largely indifferent to most international concerns. They firmly discounted the likelihood of American involvement in another major war, except perhaps with Japan. Isolationist strength in Congress led to the passage of the Neutrality Act of 1937, making it unlawful for the United States to trade with belligerents. American policy aimed at continental defense and designated the Navy as the first line of such defense. The Army's role was to serve as the nucleus of a mass mobilization that would defeat any invaders who managed to fight their way past the Navy and the nation's powerful coastal defense installations. The National Defense Act of 1920 allowed an Army of 280,000, the largest in peacetime history, but until 1939 Congress never appropriated funds to pay for much more than half of that strength. Most of the funds available for new equipment went to the fledgling air corps. Throughout most of the interwar period, the Army was tiny and insular, filled with hard-bitten, long-serving volunteers scattered in small garrisons throughout the continental United States, Hawaii, the Philippines, and Panama.

Yet some innovative thinking and preparation for the future took place in the interwar Army. Experiments with armored vehicles and motorization, air-ground cooperation, and the aerial transport of troops came to nothing for lack of resources and of consistent high-level support. The Army did, however, develop an interest in amphibious warfare and in related techniques that were then being pioneered by the U.S. Marine Corps. By the outbreak of war the Signal Corps was a leader in improving radio communications, and American artillery practiced the most sophisticated fire-direction and -control techniques in the world. In addition, war plans for various contingencies had been drawn up, as had industrial and manpower mobilization plans. During the early 1930s Col. George C. Marshall, assistant commandant of the Infantry School at Fort Benning, Georgia, had earmarked a number of younger officers for leadership positions. Despite such preparations, the Army as a whole was unready for the war that broke out in Europe on 1 September 1939.

The Outbreak of War

During March 1938 German troops had occupied Austria, incorporating it into the Reich. In September Hitler announced that the "oppression" of ethnic Germans living in Czechoslovakia was intolerable and that war was near. England and France met with Hitler (the Munich Pact) and compelled Czechoslovakia to cede its frontier districts to Germany in order to secure "peace in our time." Peace, however, was only an illusion. During March 1939 Hitler seized the rest of Czechoslovakia by force of arms and then turned his attention to Poland. Although Britain and France had guaranteed the integrity of Poland, Hitler and Josef Stalin, dictator of the Soviet Union, signed a secret, mutual nonaggression pact in August 1939. With the pact Stalin bought time to build up his strength at the expense of Britain and France, and Hitler gained a free hand to deal with Poland. When Hitler's army invaded Poland on 1 September 1939, World War II began.

While German forces overran western Poland, Soviet troops entered from the east to claim their portion of that country. France and Britain declared war on Germany and mobilized their forces. The subsequent period of deceptive inactivity, lasting until spring, became known as the Phony War. Nothing happened to indicate that World War II would differ significantly in style or tempo from World War I.

But the years since 1918 had brought important developments in the use of tanks. A number of students of war—the British Sir Basil Liddell Hart and J. F. C. Fuller, the Frenchman Charles de Gaulle, the American George S. Patton, and the Germans Oswald Lutz and Heinz Guderian—believed that armored vehicles held the key to restoring decision to the battlefield. But only the Germans conceived the idea of massing tanks in division-size units, with infantry, artillery, engineers, and other supporting arms mechanized and all moving at the same pace. Moreover, only Lutz and Guderian received the enthusiastic support of their government.

In the spring of 1940 their theories were put to the test as German forces struck against Norway and Denmark in April; invaded the Netherlands, Belgium, and Luxembourg in May; and late in the same month broke through a hilly, wooded district in France. Their columns sliced through to the English Channel, cutting off British and French troops in northern France and Belgium. The French Army, plagued by low morale, divided command, and primitive communications, fell apart. The British evacuated their forces from Dunkerque with the loss of most of their equipment. The Germans entered Paris on 14 June, and the French government, defeatist and deeply divided politically, sued for an armistice. The success of the German *Blitzkrieg* forced the remaining combatants to rethink their doctrine and restructure their armies.

With his forces occupying northern France and with a puppet French government established in the south, Hitler launched the *Luftwaffe* against the airfields and cities of England to pave the way for an invasion. Britain's survival hung by a thread. From July to October 1940, while German landing barges and invasion forces waited on the Channel coasts, the Royal Air Force, greatly outnumbered, drove the *Luftwaffe* from the daytime skies in the legendary Battle of Britain. At sea the British Navy, with increasing American cooperation, fought a desperate battle against German submarine packs to keep the North Atlantic open. British pugnacity finally forced Hitler to abandon all plans to invade England.

In February Hitler sent troops under Lt. Gen. Erwin Rommel to aid the Italians who were fighting against the British in North Africa. German forces coming to the aid of the Italians in the Balkans routed a British expedition in Greece, and German paratroopers seized the important island of Crete. Then, in June 1944, Hitler turned against his supposed ally, the Soviet Union, with the full might of the German armed forces.

Armored spearheads thrust deep into Soviet territory, driving toward Leningrad, Moscow, and the Ukraine and cutting off entire Soviet armies. Despite tremendous losses, Russian military forces withdrew farther into the country and continued to resist. Nazi expectations of a quick victory evaporated, and the onset of winter caught the Germans unprepared. Thirty miles short of Moscow their advance ground to a halt, and the Soviets launched massive counterattacks.

The Germans withstood the counterattacks and resumed their offensive the following spring. The Soviets, now locked in a titanic death struggle, faced the bulk of the German land forces—over two hundred divisions. The front stretched for 2,000 miles, from the Arctic Circle to the Black Sea. Soon casualties ran into the millions. Waging war with the implacable ruthlessness of totalitarian regimes, both sides committed wholesale atrocities—mistreatment of prisoners of war, enslavement of civilian populations, and, in the case of the Jews, outright genocide.

In the United States preparations for war moved slowly. General George C. Marshall took over as Chief of Staff in 1939, but the Army remained hard pressed simply to carry out its mission of defending the continental United States. Defending overseas possessions like the Philippines seemed a hopeless task. In early 1939, prompted by fears that a hostile power might be able to establish air bases in the Western Hemisphere, thus exposing the Panama Canal or continental United States to aerial attack, President Franklin D. Roosevelt launched a limited preparedness campaign. The power of the Army Air Corps increased; Army and Navy leaders drafted a new series of war plans to deal with the threatening international situation. The focus of military policy changed from continental to hemisphere defense.

After the outbreak of war in Europe the President proclaimed a limited emergency and authorized increases in the size of the Regu-

"Barrage Balloon" by Alexander Brook. The reported ability of balloons to interfere with low-level bombardment in Great Britain and Germany spurred the Army to develop a barrage balloon force for continental defense. (Army Art Collection)

lar Army and the National Guard. Congress amended the Neutrality Act to permit munitions sales to the French and British, and large orders from them stimulated retooling and laid the basis for the expansion of war production in the future. The Army concentrated on equipping its regular forces as quickly as possible and in 1940 held the first large-scale corps and army maneuvers in American history.

The rapid defeat of France and the possible collapse of Britain dramatically accelerated defense preparations. Roosevelt directed the transfer of large stocks of World War I munitions to France and Britain in the spring of 1940 and went further in September when he agreed to the transfer of fifty over-age destroyers to Britain in exchange for bases in the Atlantic and Caribbean. In March 1941 Congress repealed some provisions of the Neutrality Act. Passage of the Lend-Lease Act, which gave the President authority to sell, transfer, or lease war goods to the government of any country whose defenses he deemed vital to the defense of the United States, spelled the virtual end of neutrality. The President proclaimed that the United States would become the "arsenal of democracy." In the spring of 1941 American and British military representatives held their first combined staff conferences to discuss strategy in the event of active U.S. participation in the war, which seemed increasingly likely to include Japan as well as Germany. The staffs agreed that if the United States entered the war the Allies should concentrate on the defeat of Germany first. The President authorized active naval patrols in the western half of the Atlantic, and in July, American troops took the place of British forces guarding Iceland.

Meanwhile, General Marshall and Secretary of War Henry L. Stimson made plans to expand the Army to 1.5 million men. On 27 August 1940, Congress approved inducting the National Guard into federal service and calling up the reserves. A few weeks later the lawmakers passed the Selective Service and Training Act, the first peacetime draft in American history. By mid-1941 the Army had achieved its planned strength, with 27 infantry, 5 armored, and 2 cavalry divisions; 35 air groups; and a host of support units. But it remained far from ready to deploy overseas against well-equipped, experienced, and determined foes.

The United States Enters the War

On 7 December 1941, while German armies were freezing before Moscow, Japan suddenly pushed the United States into the struggle by attacking the American naval base at Pearl Harbor, Hawaii. Four days later Hitler declared war on the United States. President Roosevelt called on Congress for immediate and massive expansion of the armed forces. Twenty years of neglect and indifference, however, could not be overcome in a few days.

Helpless as American garrisons in the Pacific fell to the Japanese in the spring of 1942, military leaders in Washington worked feverishly to create a headquarters that could direct a distant war effort and to turn the fledgling ground and air units into viable, balanced fighting forces. In early 1942 the Joint Chiefs of Staff emerged as a committee of the nation's military leaders to advise the President and to coordinate strategy with the British. In March the War Department General Staff was reorganized and the Army divided into three major commands: the Air Forces, Ground Forces, and Service Forces. Thirty-seven Army divisions were in some state of training, but only one was fully trained, equipped, and deployable by January

"Ex-Luxury Liner" by Barse Miller. The largest liners used by the Army, the British ships Queen Elizabeth *and* Queen Mary, *could each carry up to 15,000 troops.* (Army Art Collection)

1942. Army planners of the time estimated that victory would require an Army of nearly 9 million men, organized into 215 combat divisions, estimates that proved accurate regarding overall manpower but too ambitious for the 90 divisions that eventually were established and supported on far-flung battlefields.

Lt. Gen. Lesley J. McNair, head of Army Ground Forces and an ardent advocate of mobile war, oversaw the development of armored and airborne divisions. He directed the restructuring of existing organizations as well, turning the old World War I "square" division based on four infantry regiments into a lighter, more maneuverable triangular division with three infantry regiments. A serious and continuing shortage of Allied shipping space placed absolute limits on the size and capabilities of Army units. New tables of organization stressed leanness and mobility, sometimes at the expense of fighting power and endurance. Billeting, training areas, and equipment were all in short supply. American industry had to support the nation's Allies as well as its own military expansion. Britain needed large amounts of munitions and equipment; and lend-lease aid, including tens of thousands of trucks and other vehicles and equipment, played an important part in mechanizing the Soviet Army. Amphibious warfare required large numbers of landing craft and support vessels, yet to be built. The first U.S. troops arrived in the British Isles in January 1942, but nearly a year passed before they went into action against the Axis. Meanwhile, air power provided virtually the only means for the Allies to strike at Germany. The Royal Air Force began its air offensive against Germany in May 1942, and on 4 July the first American crews participated in air raids against the Continent.

In early 1942 British and American leaders reaffirmed the priority of the European theater. General Marshall argued for an immediate buildup of American forces in Great Britain, a possible diversionary attack on the Continent in the fall, and a definite full-scale invasion in 1943. The British greeted this program with caution. Remembering the enormous casualties of World War I, they preferred to strike at German power in the Mediterranean, rather than risk a direct confrontation in haste. Although acknowledging the eventual necessity for an invasion of France, they hoped to defer it until much later. Instead, Prime Minister Winston S. Churchill suggested Anglo-American landings in North Africa, bringing the French armies in France's colonies there back into the war on the side of the Allies and aiding the British in their fight against the Italians and the forces of German Field Marshal Erwin Rommel. Months of lively debate followed, but ultimately President Roosevelt directed General Marshall to plan and carry out amphibious landings on the coast of North Africa before the end of 1942.

The North African Campaign

Marshall ordered Lt. Gen. Dwight D. Eisenhower, then in England, to take command of the invasion. Meeting the November deadline required improvisation of every kind. Army troops were hurriedly trained in amphibious warfare. Technicians modified commercial vessels to serve as landing ships. While General Eisenhower monitored operations from Gibraltar, American forces, convoyed directly from the United States, landed along the Atlantic coast of French Morocco, near Casablanca. Meanwhile, American and British troops sailing from England landed in Algeria. Despite efforts to win support among French military officers in North Africa, some fighting occurred. Nevertheless negotiations soon led to a cease-fire, and French units joined the Allied forces.

While the Allies tightened their grip on Morocco and Algeria, their troops raced to reach strategic positions in neighboring Tunisia. A month earlier the British in Egypt under Lt. Gen. Sir Bernard L. Montgomery had mounted a powerful attack on the Germans at El Alamein, sending Rommel and his *German-Italian Panzer Army* reeling back into Libya. If strong Allied forces could reach the coast of Tunisia, Rommel would be trapped between them and Montgomery's troops.

Awake to the threat, the Germans poured troops into Tunisia by air and sea, brushing aside weak French forces there. Axis air power, based in Sicily, Sardinia, and Italy, pounded the advancing Allied columns. As torrential December rains turned the countryside into a quagmire, the Allies lost the race. Instead of catching Rommel, they faced a protracted struggle. While his forces dug in along the southern border of Tunisia opposite Montgomery, a second powerful Axis force, the *Fifth Panzer Army,* barred the way to the Tunisian coast.

A chain of mountains separates coastal Tunisia from the arid interior. In a plain between two arms of the mountains and behind the passes in the west lay important Allied airfields and supply dumps. On 14 February 1943, the Axis commanders sent German and Italian forces through the passes, hoping to penetrate the American positions and either envelop the British in the north or seize Allied supply de-

"Hill 609" by Fletcher Martin. Much of the Army's fighting in the final offensive in northern Tunisia involved dismounted infantry attacks on prepared defensive positions in rugged hill country. (Army Art Collection)

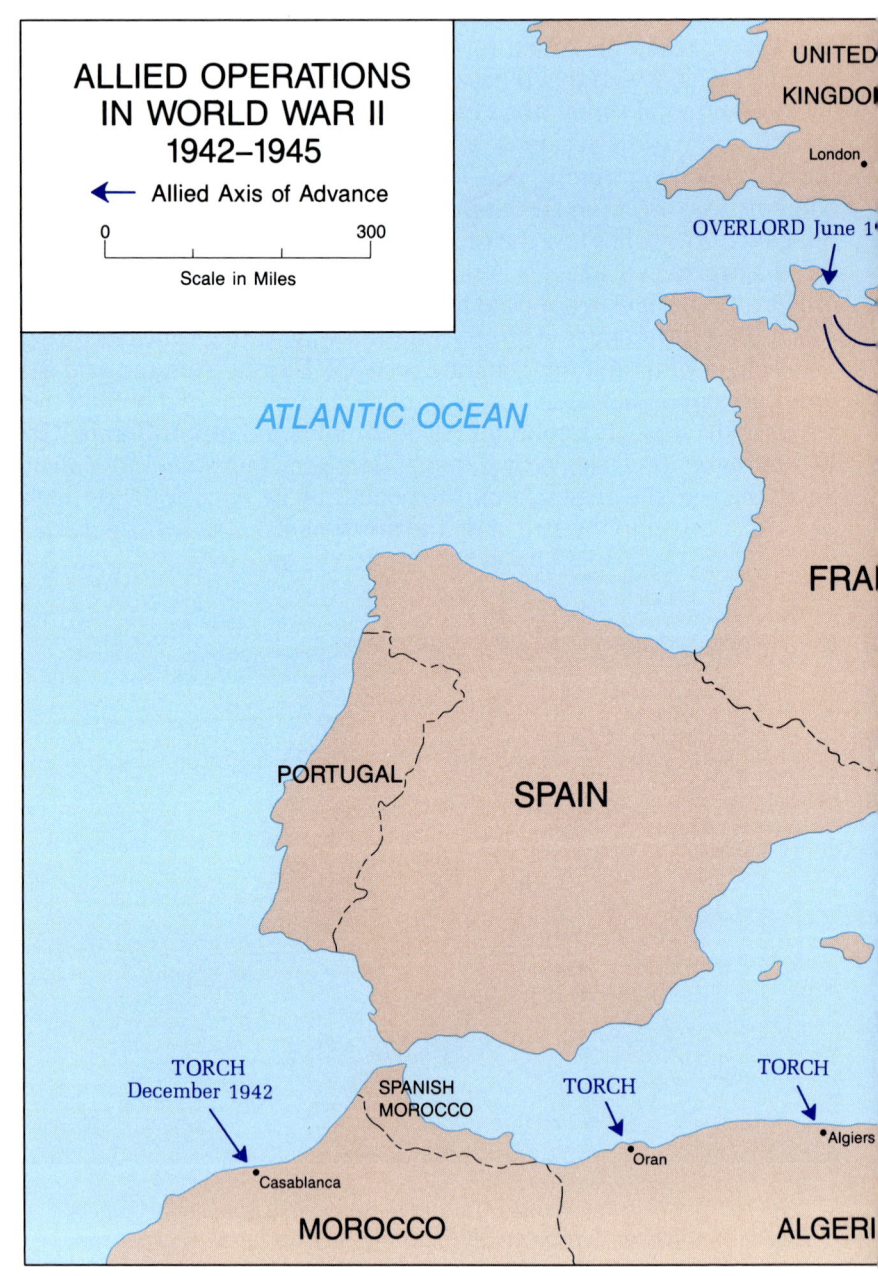

pots. German forces quickly cut off and overwhelmed two battalions of American infantry positioned too far apart for mutual support, and the experienced *panzers* beat back counterattacks by American reserves, including elements of the U.S. 1st Armored Division. U.S. troops began evacuating airfields and supply depots on the plain and falling back to the western arm of the mountains. Dug in around the oasis town of Sbeitla, American infantry and armor managed to hold off the Germans through 16 February, but defenses there began to disintegrate during the night, and the town lay empty by midday on the 17th. From the oasis, roads led back to two passes, the Sbiba and the Kasserine. By 21 February the Germans had pushed through both and were poised to seize road junctions leading to the British rear.

Rommel and other German commanders, however, could not agree on how to exploit their success. Meanwhile Allied reinforcements rushed to the critical area. The 1st Armored Division turned back German probes toward Tebessa, and British armor met a more powerful thrust toward Thala, where four battalions of field artillery from the U.S. 9th Infantry Division arrived just in time to bolster sagging defenses. On the night of 22 February the Germans began to pull back. A few days later Allied forces returned to the passes. The first American battle with German forces had cost more than 6,000 U.S. casualties, including 300 dead and two-thirds of the tank strength of the 1st Armored Division.

In March, after the British repulsed another German attack, the Allies resumed the offensive. The U.S. II Corps, now under the command of Maj. Gen. George S. Patton, attacked in coordination with an assault on the German line by Montgomery's troops. American and British forces in the south met on 7 April as they squeezed Axis forces into the northeastern tip of the country. The final drive to clear Tunisia began on 19 April. On 7 May British armor entered Tunis, and American infantry entered Bizerte. Six days later the last Axis resistance in Africa ended with the surrender of over 275,000 prisoners of war.

The U.S. Army learned bitter lessons about the inadequacy of its training, equipment, and leadership in the North African campaign. Army Ground Forces acted quickly to ensure that American soldiers would receive more realistic combat training. Higher commanders realized that they could not interfere with their subordinates by dictating in detail the positions of their units. Troops had to be committed in division-size, combined arms teams, not in driblets. The problem posed by American tanks, outgunned by the more heavily armed and armored German *panzers*, took far longer to correct. But the artillery established itself as the Army's most proficient arm.

Sicily and Italy

Meeting in Casablanca in January 1943, President Roosevelt, Prime Minister Churchill, and the Combined Chiefs of Staff decided that the large Italian island of Sicily would be their next target. Montgomery's British forces landed on the southeast coast, while Patton's newly activated Seventh Army landed on the southwest, with the mission of seizing airfields and protecting the flank of the British drive. Airborne troops spearheading the attacks scattered wide of their targets but managed to disrupt enemy communications. Hours after the initial landings on 9 July, German armor struck the American beaches. Naval gunfire, infantry counterattacks, and the direct fire of field artillery landing at the critical juncture broke up the German formations. But two attempts to reinforce the beaches with parachute and glider-borne troops ended in disaster when Allied antiaircraft batteries mistook the transport planes for enemy aircraft and opened fire, causing severe losses.

Meanwhile, the Germans solidly blocked the British drive on the Sicilian capital, Messina. General Sir Harold R. L. G. Alexander, Allied ground commander, ordered Patton to push toward Palermo, at the western tip of the island. Once in Palermo, since the British drive was still stalled, his forces attacked Messina from the north. Patton used a series of small amphibious end runs to outflank German positions on the northern coastal road. American and British troops arrived in Messina on 17 August, just as the last Axis troops evacuated Sicily.

In late July the Allies decided to follow up their success in Sicily with an invasion of Italy. Having lost hope of victory, the *Italian High Command*, backed by the king, opened secret negotiations with the Allies. The Germans, suspecting that Italy was about to desert the Axis, rushed in additional troops.

The Germans swiftly disarmed the *Italian Army* and took over its defensive positions. A British fleet sailed into the harbor of Taranto and disembarked troops onto the docks, while the U.S. Fifth Army under Lt. Gen. Mark W. Clark landed on the beaches near Salerno on 9 September. The Germans reacted in strength. For four days vigorous attacks by German armor threatened the beaches. But on 16 September American and British forces made contact, and two weeks later American troops entered Naples, the largest city south of Rome. Allied plans called for a continued advance to tie down German troops and prevent their transfer to France or Russia, while Hitler decided to hold as much of Italy as possible.

"Bailey Bridge" by Tom Craig. Mechanized warfare demanded a substantial increase in tactical bridging; in Italy the Bailey Bridge proved versatile and adaptable to a variety of weights and situations. (Army Art Collection)

As the Allies advanced up the mountainous spine of Italy, they confronted a series of heavily fortified German defensive positions, anchored on rivers or commanding terrain features. The brilliant delaying tactics of the German commander in Italy, Field Marshal Albert Kesselring, exacted a high price for every Allied gain. The campaign in Italy became an endless siege, fought in rugged terrain, in often appalling conditions, and with limited resources.

Moving north from Naples, the Allies forced a crossing of the Volturno River in October 1943 and advanced to the Winter Line, a main German defensive position anchored on mountains around Cassino. Repeated attempts over the next six months to break or outflank it failed. An amphibious end run, landing the U.S. VI Corps under Maj. Gen. John P. Lucas at Anzio in January 1944, failed to turn the German flank, for Lucas waited too long to build up his reserves before moving aggressively against the German defenses. Kesselring had time to call in reinforcements, including artillery, which soon brought every inch of Allied-held ground under fire. As the defenders dug in, the end run turned into another siege, as American and British troops repulsed repeated counterattacks.

Meanwhile, an American attempt to cross the Rapido River, timed to coincide with the Anzio landing, miscarried with heavy casualties. Allied efforts to blast a way through the enemy's mountain defenses proved futile, despite the use of medium and heavy bombers to support ground attacks around Cassino. Finally, in May 1944, a series of coordinated attacks by the Fifth Army and Eighth Army pried the Germans loose, and they began to fall back. On 4 June 1944, two days before the Normandy invasion, Allied troops entered Rome.

The Normandy invasion made Italy a secondary theater, and Allied strength there gradually decreased. Nevertheless, the fighting continued. The Allies attacked a new German defensive line in the Northern Appenines in August but were unable to make appreciable headway through the mountains. Not until spring of 1945 did they penetrate the final German defenses and enter the Po valley. German forces in Italy surrendered on 2 May 1945.

The Cross-Channel Attack

Preparations for an attack on German-occupied France continued as did the campaigns in the Mediterranean. The defeat of the German U-boat threat, critical to the successful transport of men and materiel across the Atlantic, had been largely accomplished by the second half of 1943. The success of the war against the U-boats was immeasurably aided by secret intelligence, code-named ULTRA, garnered by Anglo-American breaking of German radio communications codes. Such information also proved valuable to the commanders of the ground campaign in Italy and France.

By early 1944 an Allied strategic bombing campaign so reduced German strength in fighters and trained pilots that the Allies effectively established complete air superiority over western Europe. Allied bombers now turned to systematic disruption of the transportation system in France in order to impede the enemy's ability to respond to the invasion. At the same time, American and British leaders orchestrated a tremendous buildup in the British Isles, transporting 1.6 million men and their equipment to England and providing them with shelter and training facilities.

Detailed planning for the cross-Channel assault had begun in 1943 when the American and British Combined Chiefs of Staff appointed a British officer, Lt. Gen. Frederick E. Morgan, as Chief of Staff to the as yet unnamed Supreme Allied Commander. When General Eisenhower arrived in January 1944 to set up Supreme Headquarters, Allied Expeditionary Force (SHAEF), Morgan's work served as the basis for the final plan of assault. The Allies would land in Normandy and seize the port of Cherbourg. They would establish an expanded lodgment area extending as far east as the Seine River. Having built up reserves there, they would then advance into Germany on a broad front. Ground commander for the invasion would be General Montgomery. The British Second Army would land on the left, while the American First Army, under Lt. Gen. Omar N. Bradley, landed on the right. Intensive exercises and rehearsals occupied the last months before the invasion. An elaborate deception plan convinced the Germans that the Normandy landings were a feint, and that larger, more important landings would take place farther east, around the Pas de Calais. Here the Germans held most of their reserves, keeping their armored formations near Paris.

Developments on the Eastern Front also aided the success of the invasion. In early 1943 the Russians destroyed a German army at Stalingrad. The Germans tried to regain the initiative in the summer of 1943, attacking a Soviet-held salient near the Russian city of Kursk. In the largest tank battle known to history, they suffered a resounding defeat. Henceforth, they remained on the defensive, in constant retreat, while the Soviets advanced westward, retaking major portions of the Ukraine and White Russia during the fall and winter and launching an offensive around Leningrad in January 1944. By March 1944 Soviet forces had reentered Polish territory, and a Soviet summer offensive had prevented the Germans from transferring troops to France.

"Sherman Tanks Passing Stream of German Prisoners" by Ogden Pleissner. After seven weeks of slow, costly advances against determined German defenders in the hedgerows, Army armored formations seized the initiative at St. Lo and made rapid advances against a demoralized enemy. (Army Art Collection)

On 5 June 1944, General Eisenhower took advantage of a break in stormy weather to order the invasion of "fortress Europe." In the hours before dawn, 6 June 1944, one British and two U.S. airborne divisions dropped behind the beaches. After sunrise, British, Canadian, and U.S. troops began to move ashore. The British and Canadians met modest opposition. Units of the U.S. VII Corps quickly broke through defenses at a beach code-named UTAH and began moving inland, making contact with the airborne troops within twenty-four hours. But heavy German fire swept OMAHA, the other American landing area. Elements of the 1st and 29th Infantry Divisions and the 2d and 5th Ranger Battalions clung precariously to a narrow stretch of stony beach until late in the day, when they were finally able to advance, outflanking the German positions.

American and British beachheads linked up within days. While the Allies raced to build up supplies and reserves, American and British fighter aircraft and guerrillas of the French resistance blocked movement of German reinforcements. On the ground, Allied troops besieged Cherbourg and struggled to expand southward through the entangling Norman hedgerows. Earthen embankments hundreds of years old, matted with the roots of trees and shrubs, the hedgerows divided the countryside into thousands of tiny fields. The narrow roads, sunk beneath the level of the surrounding countryside, became deathtraps for tanks and vehicles. Crossroads villages were clusters of solidly built medieval stone buildings, ideal for defense. Small numbers of German infantry, dug into the embankments with machine guns and mortars and a tank or two or a few antitank guns for support, made advancing across each field costly.

With time short and no room to maneuver, the struggle to break out became a battle of attrition. Allied troops advanced with agonizing slowness from hedgerow to hedgerow, in a seemingly endless series of small battles. Advances were measured in hundreds of yards. Requirements for fire support far exceeded preinvasion planning, resulting in a severe shortage of artillery shells. The British made several powerful attempts to break through to the open country beyond the town of Caen, but were stopped by the Germans, who concentrated most of their armor in this threatened area. By 18 July the U.S. First Army had clawed its way into St. Lo and, on 25 July, launched Operation COBRA. As heavy and medium bombers from England pummeled German frontline positions, infantry and armor finally punched through the defenses. Pouring through the gap, American troops advanced forty miles within a week.

Rejecting his generals' advice, Hitler ordered a counterattack against the widening breakout by Germany's last available mobile forces in France. U.S. First Army forces stopped the Germans and joined Canadian, British, and Polish troops in catching the enemy in a giant pocket around the town of Falaise. Allied fighter bombers and artillery now aided a massive destruction of twenty enemy divisions. Suddenly, it seemed the Allies might end the war before winter. Calling off a planned halt and logistical buildup, Eisenhower ordered the Allied forces to drive all-out for the German frontier.

With enemy forces in full retreat, French and American troops rolled into Paris on 25 August 1944. Meanwhile, veteran U.S. and French divisions, pulled out of Italy, landed on the beaches of the French Riviera. While French forces liberated the ports, the U.S. Seventh Army drove northward in an effort to cut off withdrawing German troops. Moving rapidly through the cities of Lyon and Besancon, they joined up with Allied forces advancing from Normandy on 11 September.

Victory seemed to be at hand. But by mid-September Allied communications were strained. Combat troops had outrun their supplies. British and Canadian forces advanced into the Netherlands, and American troops crossed Belgium and Luxembourg and entered German territory. Then both met strong resistance. Bad weather curtailed unloading of supplies directly across the Normandy invasion beaches, while the ports on the North Sea and the Mediterranean were in ruins. As logistical problems piled up, Eisenhower rejected as too dangerous British pleas to channel all available resources into one deep thrust into Germany. He did, however, sanction one last bold gamble: Operation MARKET-GARDEN. Two U.S. and one British airborne division were to open the way for a British armored thrust to seize a bridge across the lower Rhine at Arnhem in the Netherlands. The airborne troops took most of their objectives, but German resistance was much stronger than expected, and the operation failed to gain a bridgehead across the Rhine.

Battles of Attrition

There was to be no early end to the war. Despite its recent defeats, the *German Army* remained a dangerous foe, fighting for its life in prepared defenses. Furthermore, as the Allies approached the frontiers of the Reich, they encountered a series of formidable terrain obstacles—major rivers, mountains, and forests—and the worst weather in over thirty years. Yet Eisenhower, believing that unremitting pressure against the enemy would shorten the war, called for the offensive to continue. Battles of attrition followed throughout October and November, all along the front.

Canadian and British soldiers trudged through the frozen mud and water of the flooded tidal lowlands in the Netherlands to free the great Belgian port of Antwerp. The U.S. First Army took the German city of Aachen on 21 October. The drive of General Patton's Third Army toward the German border halted on 25 September due to shortages of gasoline and other critical supplies. Resuming the offensive in November, Patton's men fought for two bloody weeks around the fortress town of Metz, ultimately winning bridgeheads over the Saar River and probing the Siegfried Line. In the south the U.S. Seventh Army and the First French Army fought their way through the freezing rain and snow of the Vosges Mountains to break out onto the Alsatian plain around Strasbourg, becoming the only Allied armies to reach the Rhine in 1944. But there were no strategic objectives directly east of Strasbourg, and a pocket of tough German troops remained on the west bank, dug in around the old city of Colmar.

The attacks by the U.S. First and Ninth Armies toward the Roer River were extremely difficult. The Huertgen Forest through which they moved was thickly wooded, cut by steep defiles, fire breaks, and trails. The Germans built deep, artillery-proof log bunkers, surrounded by fighting positions. They placed thousands of mines in the forest. In addition, they felled trees across the roads and wired, mined, and booby-trapped them; and registered their artillery, mortars, and machine guns on the roadblocks. Tree-high artillery bursts, spewing thousands of lethal splinters, made movement on the forest floor difficult. Armor had no room to maneuver. Two months of bloody, close-quarters fighting in mud, snow, and cold was devastating to morale. Parts of at least three U.S. divisions, pushed beyond all human limits, experienced breakdowns of cohesion and discipline.

The Battle of the Bulge

While the Allies bludgeoned their way into the border marches of the Reich, Hitler carefully husbanded Germany's last reserves of tanks and infantry for a desperate attempt to reverse the situation in the west. On 16 December powerful German forces struck the lightly held sector of the First Army front south of Monschau in the Ardennes. German armored spearheads drove toward the Meuse River, aiming at Antwerp. Aided by bad weather, a variety of deceptive measures, and the failure of Allied intelligence correctly to interpret the signs of an impending attack, they achieved complete surprise. Elements of five U.S. divisions plus support troops fell back in confusion. Two regiments of the 106th Infantry Division, cut off and surrounded atop the mountainous Schnee Eiffel, surrendered after only brief fighting—the largest battlefield surrender of U.S. troops in World War II.

Partly as a result of the decision to continue attacking throughout the autumn, U.S. forces were spread thin in areas such as the Ardennes, and the Americans had few reserves to meet the attack. SHAEF immediately ordered available units into the threatened area, sending an airborne division into the important communications center of Bastogne. By 18 December the magnitude of the German effort was clear, and Eisenhower ordered Patton's Third Army to disengage from its offensive toward the Saar and to attack the enemy's southern flank. Scattered American units, fighting desperate rearguard actions, disrupted the German timetable, obstructing or holding key choke points—road junctions, narrow defiles, and single-lane bridges across unfordable streams—to buy time. Defenders at the town of St. Vith held out for six days; V Corps troops at Elsenborn Ridge repelled furious attacks, jamming the northern shoulder of the enemy advance. To the south armored and airborne troops, although completely surrounded and under heavy German attack, held Bastogne for the duration of the battle. German efforts to widen the southern shoulder of the bulge along the Sauer River came to nothing.

Short of fuel, denied critical roadnets, hammered by air attacks, and confronted by American armor, the German spearheads recoiled short of the Meuse. Meanwhile, Patton had altered the Third Army's axis of advance and attacked northward, relieving Bastogne on 26 December. On 3 January First and Ninth Army troops and British forces launched attacks against the northern shoulder of the bulge. Meanwhile, a secondary German offensive, Operation *NORDWIND*, failed in the south. Eisenhower had ordered the Sixth Army Group to fall back, pulling out of Strasbourg. General de Gaulle, the French leader, was enraged. After heated negotiations, Allied troops remained in Strasbourg, and the German attack lost its momentum. By the end of January the Allies had retaken all the ground lost in both German offensives. The Battle of the Bulge was over.

Just as the Allies' August breakout had failed to achieve a war-winning decision, so, too, the German attempt to reenact its victory of June 1940 failed. The Allies, however, could make good their losses, while Hitler had squandered almost all his remaining armor and fighter aircraft. To make matters worse for the Reich, the Soviets on 12 January opened a large-scale offensive in Poland and East Prussia that carried their troops to within forty miles of Berlin. German forces that survived the Ardennes fighting had to be hurriedly shifted eastward to meet the growing Russian threat.

The Final Offensive

With the elimination of the "bulge" and the repulse of *NORDWIND*, the campaign in the west moved into its final phases. The Allies paused only briefly before resuming the offensive. Eisenhower had earlier decided that his armies should advance to the Rhine all along its length before crossing; he wanted to shorten Allied lines, provide a defensible position in the event of further German counterattacks, and free troops to build up strong reserves. If Hitler persisted in defending every inch of German territory, most of the enemy's remaining forces would be destroyed west of the Rhine. Once across the river, American and British forces would be able to advance into Germany almost at will.

Harmonizing conflicting British and American views remained one of Eisenhower's major problems. Rejecting British proposals to concentrate on one thrust north of the Ruhr under Montgomery's leadership, Eisenhower planned concentric attacks from the north by the British 21 Army Group and the U.S. Ninth Army and from the south by the U.S. First Army. Meanwhile, the Third Army would drive straight across Germany, and the Seventh Army would turn southward into Bavaria. Because the United States now dominated the alliance, most of the significant tasks of the final campaign went to American commanders.

First, a pocket of German resistance at Colmar had to be eliminated. Eisenhower assigned five additional U.S. divisions and 10,000 service troops to the effort. The Franco-American attack against the pocket began on 20 January and was over by early February. Meantime, the Canadian First Army cleared the area between the Maas and Rhine Rivers. At the same time, the First Army advanced and finally seized the Roer River dams but found that the Germans had destroyed the controls. The resultant flooding delayed the Ninth Army's advance by two weeks. That attack finally began in late February and linked up with the Canadians, cutting off German forces facing the British. Meanwhile, the First Army's drive to the Rhine culminated in the capture of Cologne and on 7 March the seizure of an intact bridge at the town of Remagen.

As American divisions poured into the bridgehead, the Third and Seventh Armies launched coordinated attacks to the south. On the 22d and the 25th, Third Army troops made assault crossings of the Rhine. On 23 March the British Second Army and the U.S. Ninth Army staged massive crossings in the Rees-Wesel–Dinslaken area, supported by the largest airborne landings of the war, while the Seventh Army crossed on the 26th near Worms. Now Allied columns fanned out across Germany, overrunning isolated pockets of resistance. While Montgomery's forces drove northward toward the great German ports of Bremen, Hamburg, and Luebeck, the Ninth Army advanced along the axis Muenster-Magdeburg. Ninth and First Army troops met on 1 April, encircling the industrial region of the Ruhr and capturing 325,000 prisoners. The First Army continued eastward toward Kassel and Leipzig while the Third Army rolled through Frankfurt, Eisenach, and Erfurt toward Dresden, then southward toward Czechoslovakia and Austria. The Sixth Army Group advanced into Bavaria toward Munich and Salzburg, denying the Germans a last-ditch defense in the Bavarian or Austrian Alps. Germany was shattered.

Nevertheless, Eisenhower resisted British pressure to drive on to Berlin. He saw no point in taking casualties to capture ground that, in line with earlier agreements between Allied leaders, would have to be relinquished to the Soviets once hostilities ceased. His objective remained to capture or destroy the remnants of the German armed forces. The Soviets massed 1.2 million men and 22,000 pieces of artillery and on 16 April began their assault upon the city. As that battle raged, British, American, and Soviet forces neared previously negotiated stop lines along the Elbe and Mulde Rivers. The First Army made contact with Soviet troops on 25 April around Torgau. Meanwhile, as the Third Army entered Czechoslovakia and British troops reached the Baltic, the Russians moved through the streets of Berlin. On 30 April 1945, Hitler committed suicide in a bunker beneath the ruins of his capitol.

German forces in Italy surrendered effective 2 May and those in the Netherlands, northwestern Germany, and Denmark on 4 May. Patrols of the U.S. Seventh Army driving eastward through Austria and the Fifth Army driving north from Italy met near the Brenner Pass. On 7 May the *German High Command* surrendered all its forces unconditionally, and 8 May was officially proclaimed V–E Day. Though peace had come to Europe, one of the most culturally and economically advanced areas of the globe lay in ruins. Germany, the industrial engine of the Continent, lay prostrate, occupied by British, French, American, and Soviet troops. Britain, exhausted by its contribution to the victory, tottered near economic collapse, while France was totally dependent on the United States. The Soviet Union had suffered in excess of 20 million casualties and untold devastation, but its armed forces remained powerful and its intentions obscure. To the victory in western Europe and Italy, the United States had contributed 68 divisions, 15,000 combat aircraft, well over 1 million tanks and motor vehicles, and 135,000 dead. The country now turned its focus to a war a half a world away and to the defeat of Japan in the Pacific.

"Follow Me" by H. Charles McBarron. Amphibious assaults by Army and Marine infantry characterized the war in the Pacific. (Army Art Collection)

The Pacific War

The Pacific War

Even before Pearl Harbor, President Franklin D. Roosevelt and the American military chiefs had agreed on a common strategy with Great Britain: Germany, the most powerful and dangerous of the Axis powers, must be defeated first. Only enough military resources would be devoted to the Pacific to hold the Japanese west of an Alaska-Hawaii-Panama defensive line.

Competition for limited resources between the Allied commanders of the European and Pacific theaters was actually less intense than might have been expected. The Pacific was a naval war, and little U.S. offensive naval power was required in the Atlantic besides landing craft. Aside from the U-boats, the Germans posed no threat in Atlantic waters. U-boat defense primarily required many small, fast escort vessels. Then too, almost the entire British Navy was deployed in the Atlantic. Thus, American offensive naval power—especially the fast carrier task forces—could be committed to the Pacific war.

More than distance separated the two wars; they differed fundamentally in strategy and command and in the character of the fighting. In Europe the war was planned and conducted in combination with powerful Allies. Strategic decisions had to be argued and agreed to by the American and British chiefs of staff, and, on occasion, even by President Roosevelt and Prime Minister Winston Churchill. Operational planning was conducted, at least at the higher levels, by combined Anglo-American staffs. In the Pacific the United States also had Allies—Australia and New Zealand. Yet the ratio of U.S. to Allied forces was much higher there than in Europe, and in consequence strategy and planning were almost wholly in American hands.

Eisenhower, the Supreme Commander in Europe, had no counterpart in the Pacific. From the beginning of the war, rivalry between the Army and the Navy marked the conflict. The two services competed for command, territory, and resources. In the vast Pacific, an ocean dotted with thousands of coral islands, there should have been ample room for both. But interservice rivalries and great distances prevented a single unified commander from being named, until General Douglas MacArthur became Supreme Commander,

"West Coast Dock" by Barse Miller. Roughly 40 percent of the cargo moved overseas by the Army during the war went to the Pacific theater. (Army Art Collection)

Allied Powers (SCAP), in the last days of the war. Instead, the Pacific was divided into area commands. The two most important were MacArthur's Southwest Pacific Area (SWPA) and Admiral Chester Nimitz's Pacific Ocean Areas (POA). POA, in turn, was subdivided into North Pacific, Central Pacific, and South Pacific commands. Nimitz personally retained command of the Central Pacific.

Fighting in the Pacific was unlike fighting in Europe. The campaigns in Europe were characterized by huge ground forces driving overland into the heart of the enemy's country. Both in MacArthur's SWPA and Nimitz's POA, the Pacific war was a seemingly endless series of amphibious landings and island-hopping campaigns where naval power, air power, and shipping, rather than large and heavy ground forces, were of paramount importance.

Yet for the soldiers and marines who assaulted the countless beaches, the Pacific war was even more brutal and deadly than the war in Europe. Japanese defenders always dug in, reinforced their bunkers with coconut logs, and fought until they were killed. They almost never surrendered. On Betio in the Tarawa Atoll in November 1943 the marines suffered

3,301 casualties, including 900 killed in action, for a bit of coral 3 miles long and 800 yards wide. At Iwo Jima in February and March 1945 the marines lost almost 6,000 dead and over 17,000 wounded and fought for five weeks to take an island less than five miles long. At Iwo no battalion suffered fewer than 50 percent casualties, and many sustained even higher losses. In the southwest Pacific, MacArthur's casualties were proportionately fewer. Fighting on the larger land masses of New Guinea and the Philippines, he had more room to maneuver, and he could almost always "hit 'em where they ain't."

The history of the war in the Pacific falls neatly into three periods. The first six months of the war, from December 1941 to May 1942, were a time of unbroken Japanese military victory. At the height of Japanese expansion in mid-1942, the tide turned. The period from mid-1942 to mid-1943 saw Japanese strategic thrusts into the south and central Pacific blunted by the carrier battles of the Coral Sea (May 1942) and Midway (June 1942). Limited U.S. offensives in the Solomons and in the Papuan area of eastern New Guinea were launched in the last months of 1942. Both offensives were begun on a shoestring, and both came close to failure. Yet they represented the end of defeat in the Pacific and the first tentative steps toward victory. Those steps became great leaps in 1944 and 1945. Two amphibious offensives developed, as MacArthur advanced across the northern coast of New Guinea into the Philippines and Nimitz island-hopped 2,000 miles across the central Pacific from the Gilbert Islands to Okinawa.

Japan on the Offensive

Japan, largely devoid of natural resources to feed its industries, looked overseas for supplies of strategic materials such as ores and petroleum. Before 1939 the United States was Japan's major supplier. But President Roosevelt and Secretary of State Cordell Hull shut off American supplies in an effort to force the Japanese to end hostilities against China. The Japanese had long coveted the resource-rich British and Dutch colonies of Southeast Asia, and as the U.S. trade embargo tightened, the Japanese increasingly looked southward for raw materials and strategic resources.

Only the United States stood in Japan's path. The U.S. Pacific Fleet at Pearl Harbor was the only force capable of challenging Japan's navy, and American bases in the Philippines could threaten lines of communications between the Japanese home islands and the East Indies. Every oil tanker heading for Japan would have to pass by American-held Luzon. From these needs and constraints, Japan's war plans emerged. First, its navy would neutralize the American fleet with a surprise attack on Pearl Harbor. Japan would also seize America's central Pacific bases at Guam and Wake islands and invade the Philippines. With American naval power crippled, Japan's military would be free to seize Burma, Malaya, Singapore, and the Dutch East Indies in a series of rapid amphibious operations. Japan would then establish a defensive ring around its newly conquered empire by fortifying islands in the south and the central Pacific. Japan's leaders were convinced that Americans, once involved in the European war, would be willing to negotiate peace in the Pacific.

To block Japanese ambitions, the United States Army had scant resources. Two small forces constituted the heart of the American land defenses in the Pacific—the garrison in the Territory of Hawaii and General Douglas MacArthur's command in the Commonwealth of the Philippines. Both were peacetime organizations, whose days were given to rounds of ceremonies, inspections, and languid training. Officers and their wives occupied evenings and weekends with rounds of social activities and golf, while the soldiers enjoyed more earthy pleasures in the bars and brothels of Honolulu or Manila.

Yet these forces would face overwhelming odds in the event of war. The thousands of islands that comprised the Philippines lay 8,000 miles from the American west coast, but only 200 miles from Japanese-held Formosa. To defend them, General MacArthur had the equivalent of two divisions of regular troops—16,000 U.S. regulars and 12,000 Philippine Scouts. He could call on additional thousands of Philippine militia, but they were untrained and ill equipped. Lt. Gen. Walter C. Short's Hawaiian command held 43,000 Army troops, including two infantry divisions, coast artillery, air corps, and support troops. Thus, in ground forces, the United States had the equivalent of three divisions in the Pacific to stand in the path of the *Imperial Japanese Army.*

American strategists had developed two plans to counter possible Japanese aggression—one for the Navy and another for the Army. The Navy planned to fight across the central Pacific for a climactic and decisive battle with the Japanese fleet. The Army saw no way to save the Philippines and favored a strategic defense along an Alaska-Hawaii-Panama line. Writing off the Philippines, however, was politically impossible, and as war drew closer frantic efforts were made to strengthen the commonwealth's defenses. Both MacArthur and Army Chief of Staff General George C. Marshall overestimated the chances of their own forces and underestimated the strength and ability of the Japanese. In particular, they grossly exaggerated the power of a new weapon, the B–17 "Flying Fortress" bomber, a few of which were rushed to the Philippines in the last days of peace.

All of the efforts proved to be too little, too late. The Japanese war plan worked to perfection. On 7 December 1941, Japan paralyzed the Pacific Fleet in its attack on Pearl Harbor. In the Philippines, Japanese fliers destroyed most of MacArthur's air force on the ground. Freed of effective opposition, Japanese forces took Burma, Malaya, Singapore, and the Dutch East Indies in rapid succession. By March 1942 the Japanese had conquered an empire. Only MacArthur's beleaguered American-Filipino army still held out on the main Philippine island of Luzon.

A Japanese army had landed in northern Luzon on 22 December 1941 and began to push southward toward Manila. At first, MacArthur was inclined to meet the Japanese on the beaches. But he had no air force, and the U.S. Navy's tiny Asiatic fleet was in no position to challenge Japan at sea. The U.S. regulars and Philippine Scouts were excellent troops but were outnumbered and without air support. Giving up his initial strategy of defeating the enemy on the beaches, MacArthur decided to withdraw to the Bataan Peninsula. There he could pursue a strategy of defense and delay, shortening his lines and using the mountainous, jungle-covered terrain to his advantage. Perhaps he could even hold out long enough for a relief force to be mounted in the United States.

But too many people crowded into Bataan, with too little food and ammunition. By March it was clear that help from the United States was not coming. Nevertheless, the American-Filipino force, wracked by dysentery and malaria, continued to fight. In March President Roosevelt ordered MacArthur to escape to Australia. He left his command to Lt. Gen. Jonathan Wainwright and to Maj. Gen. Edward King, who on 9 April was forced to surrender the exhausted and starving Bataan force. Wainwright continued to resist on the small fortified island of Corregidor in Manila Bay until 6 May under constant Japanese artillery and air bombardment. After Japanese troops stormed ashore on the island, Wainwright agreed to surrender Corregidor and all other troops in the islands. By 9 May 1942, the battle for the Philippines had ended, though many Americans and Filipinos took to the hills and continued a guerrilla war against the Japanese.

The courageous defense of Bataan had a sad and ignominious end. Marching their prisoners toward camps in northern Luzon, the Japanese denied food and water to the sick and starving men. When the weakest prisoners began to straggle, guards shot or bayoneted them and threw the bodies to the side of the road. Japanese guards may have killed 600 Americans and 10,000 Filipino prisoners. News of the Japanese attack on Pearl Harbor had outraged the American people; news of the "Bataan Death March" filled them with bitter hatred.

By May 1942 the Japanese had succeeded beyond their wildest expectations. A vast new empire had fallen into their hands so quickly, and at so little cost, that they were tempted to go further. If their forces could move into the Solomon Islands and the southern coast of New Guinea, they could threaten Australia and cut the American line of communications to MacArthur's base there. If they could occupy Midway Island, only 1,000 miles from Honolulu, they could force the American fleet to pull back to the west coast. In Japanese overconfidence lay the seeds of Japan's first major defeats.

The Tide Turns

Japanese fortunes turned sour in mid-1942. Their uninterrupted string of victories ended with history's first great carrier battles. In May 1942 the Battle of the Coral Sea halted a new Japanese offensive in the south Pacific. A month later the Japanese suffered a devastating defeat at the Battle of Midway in the central Pacific. Now American and Australian forces were able to begin two small counteroffensives—one in the Solomons and the other on New Guinea's Papuan peninsula. The first featured the Marine Corps and the Army; the second, the Army and the Australian Allies.

American resources were indeed slim. When MacArthur arrived in Australia in March 1942, he found, to his dismay, that he had little to command. Australian militia and a few thousand U.S. airmen and service troops were his only resources. The Australian 7th Division soon returned from North Africa, where it had been fighting the Germans, and two U.S. National Guard divisions, the 32d and the 41st, arrived in April and May. MacArthur had enough planes for two bomber squadrons and six fighter squadrons. With only these forces, he set out to take Papua, while Admiral Nimitz, with forces almost equally slim, attacked Guadalcanal in the Solomon Islands.

Of all the places where GIs fought in the Second World War, Guadalcanal and the Papuan peninsula may have been the worst. Though separated by 800 miles of ocean, the two were similarly unhealthful in terrain and climate. The weather on both is perpetually hot and wet; rainfall may exceed 200 inches a year, and during the rainy season deluges, sometimes 8 to 10 inches of rain, occur daily. Temperatures in December reach the high eighties, and humidity seldom falls below 80 percent. Terrain and vegetation are equally foreboding—dark, humid,

"Bringing in the Ammo" by Joseph Hirsch. At Rendova in the Solomons, landing craft went aground in shallow water fifty feet offshore, forcing troops to wade ashore with equipment and ammunition. (Army Art Collection)

jungle-covered mountains inland, and evil-smelling swamps along the coasts. Insects abound. The soldiers and marines were never dry; most fought battles while wracked by chills and fever. For every two soldiers lost in battle, five were lost to disease—especially malaria, dengue, dysentery, or scrub typhus, a dangerous illness carried by jungle mites. Almost all suffered "jungle rot," ulcers caused by skin disease.

    Guadalcanal lay at the southeast end of the Solomons, an island chain 600 miles long. Navy carriers and other warships supported the landings, but they could not provide clear air or naval superiority. The marines landed on 7 August 1942, without opposition, and quickly overran an important airfield. That was the last easy action on Guadalcanal. The carriers sailed away almost as soon as the marines went ashore. Then Japanese warships surprised the supporting U.S. naval vessels at the Battle of Savo Island and quickly sank four heavy cruisers and one destroyer. Ashore, the *Japanese*

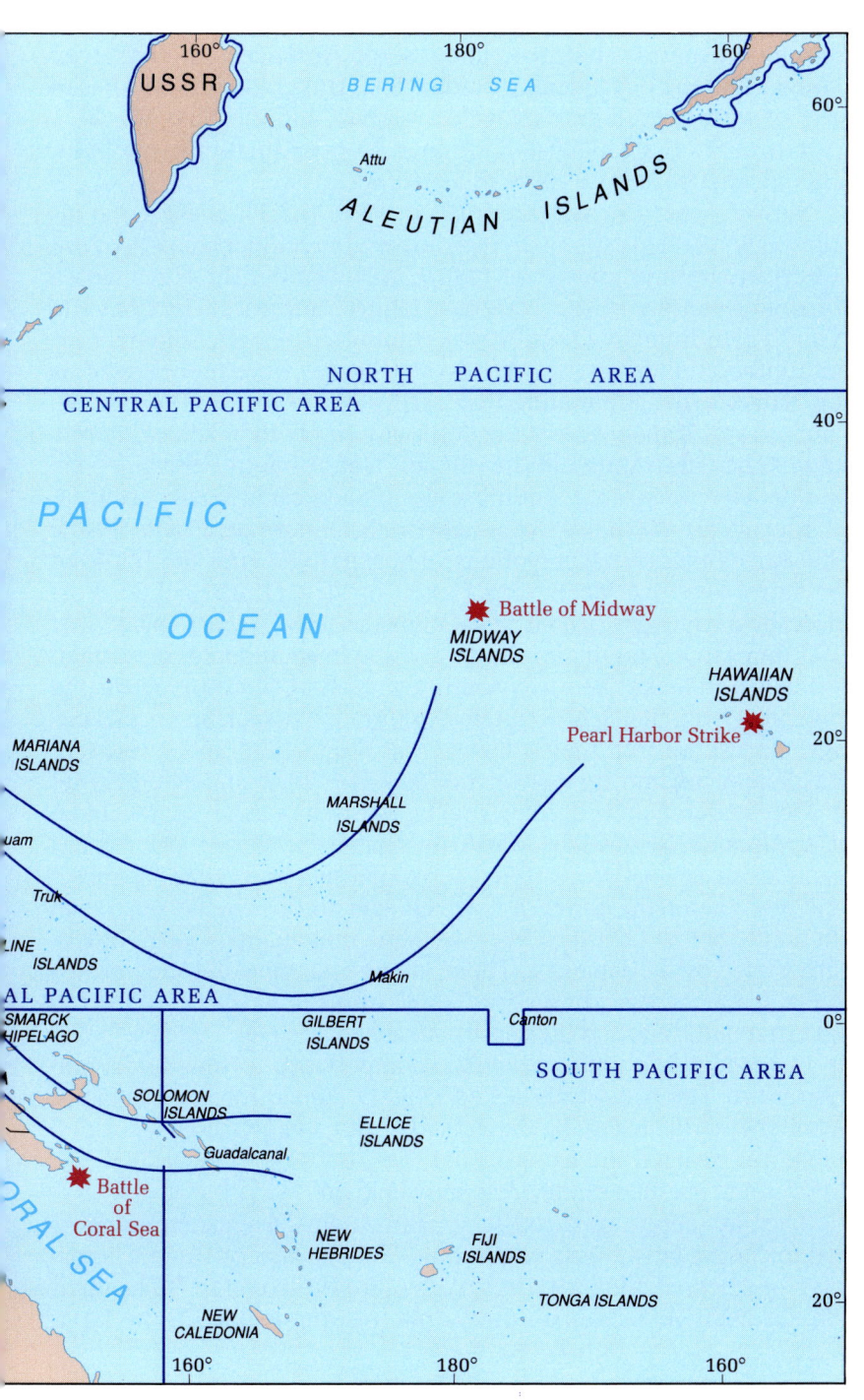

Army fought furiously to regain the airfield. Through months of fighting the marines barely held on; some American admirals even thought that the beachhead would be lost. But gradually land-based aircraft were ferried in to provide air cover, and the Navy was able to return. As the Japanese continued to pour men into the fight, Guadalcanal became a battle of attrition.

Slowly American resources grew, while the Japanese were increasingly unable to make up their losses. In October soldiers of the Americal Division joined the battle; in November the Navy won a smashing victory in the waters offshore; and in early 1943 the Army's 25th Infantry Division was committed as well. Soldiers now outnumbered marines, and the ground forces were reorganized as the XIV Corps, commanded by Army Maj. Gen. Alexander M. Patch. As the Japanese lost the ability to supply their forces, enemy soldiers began to starve in the jungles. But not until February—six months after the initial landing—was Guadalcanal finally secured.

Meanwhile, 800 miles to the west on the eastern peninsula of New Guinea, another shoestring offensive began. Even after the Battle of the Coral Sea, the Japanese persisted in their efforts to take Port Moresby, a strategic town on New Guinea's southern coast. In late July 1942 they landed on the north coast of the huge, mountainous island and began to make their way south toward Port Moresby, across the towering Owen Stanley Mountains. Almost impassable in normal circumstances, the trail they followed was a quagmire under constant rain. Supply became impossible; food ran short; fever and dysentery set in. Defeated just short of their goal by Australian defenses, the Japanese retreated. Meanwhile, MacArthur had decided to launch a counteroffensive against the fortified town of Buna and other Japanese-held positions on the northern coast. He sent portions of the Australian 7th and U.S. 32d Divisions over the same mountainous jungle tracks earlier used by the Japanese. The result was the same. By the time his troops reached the northern coast, they were almost too debilitated to fight. Around Buna and the nearby village of Gona the Japanese holed up in coconut-log bunkers that were impervious to small-arms and mortar fire. The Americans lacked artillery, flamethrowers, and tanks. While they struggled to dig the defenders out, malnutrition, fever, and jungle rot ravaged the troops. Like the troops on Guadalcanal, the Aussies and the men of the 32d barely held on.

The Japanese also faced serious problems. Their commanders had to choose between strengthening Guadalcanal or Buna. Choosing Guadalcanal, they withdrew some support from the Buna garrison. Growing American air power made it impossible for the Japanese Navy to resupply their forces ashore, and their troops began to run short of food and ammunition. By December they were on the edge of starvation. Here the battle of attrition lasted longer, and not until January 1943 was the last Japanese resistance eliminated.

Buna was costlier in casualties than Guadalcanal, and in some respects it was an even nastier campaign. The terrain was rougher; men who crossed the Owen Stanleys called that march their toughest experience of the war. The Americans lacked almost everything necessary for success—weapons, proper clothing, insect repellents, and adequate food. "No more Bunas," MacArthur pledged. For the rest of the war his policy was to bypass Japanese strongpoints. When the battles for Guadalcanal and Buna began, the Americans had insufficient strength to win. American strength increased as the battle went on. Over the next three years it would grow to overwhelming proportions.

Twin Drives to American Victory

As late as 1943 the American Joint Chiefs of Staff had not adopted a clear strategy for winning the war in the Pacific. Early in the war they assumed that the burden of the land fighting against Japan would fall on Chinese forces. The bulk of Japan's army was deployed in China, and Chinese leaders had an immense manpower pool to draw on. But supplying and training the Chinese Army proved to be an impossible task. Moreover, fighting in China did not lead to any strategic objective.

Instead, the hard-won successes in the Solomons and Papua and the growing strength of MacArthur's and Nimitz's forces gave the Joint Chiefs the means to strike at the Japanese in the Pacific. They decided to launch two converging offensives toward the Japanese islands. Using Army ground forces, land-based air power, and a fleet of old battleships and cruisers, MacArthur would leapfrog across the northern coast of New Guinea toward the Philippines. Nimitz, using carrier-based planes and Marine and Army ground forces, would island-hop across the central Pacific. The strategy was frankly opportunistic, and it left unanswered the questions of priorities and final objectives.

At the heart of the strategy were the developing techniques of amphibious warfare and tactical air power. Putting troops ashore in the face of a determined enemy had always been one of war's most dangerous and complicated maneuvers. World War II proved that the assault force needed air and sea supremacy and overwhelming combat power to be successful. Even then, dug-in defenders could take a heavy toll of infantry coming over the beaches. Special landing craft had to be built to bring tanks and artillery ashore with the

"Pim's Jetty" by Frede Vida. *The logistics of MacArthur's leaps up the New Guinea coast sometimes posed greater difficulties than did the Japanese defenders.* (Army Art Collection)

infantry, and both direct air support and effective naval gunfire were essential. MacArthur's leaps up the northern coast of New Guinea were measured precisely by the range of his fighter-bombers. The primary task of Nimitz's carriers was to support and defend the landing forces. As soon as possible after the landings, land-based planes were brought in to free the carriers for other operations.

The islands of the central Pacific had little resemblance to the fetid jungles of Guadalcanal and New Guinea. Atolls like Tarawa or Kwajalein were necklaces of hard coral surrounding lagoons of sheltered water. Where the coral rose above water, small narrow islands took form. These bits of sand furnished little room for maneuver and frequently had to be assaulted frontally. Larger islands like Guam and Saipan were volcanic in origin, with rocky ridges to aid the defense; the shrapnel effect of shell bursts was multiplied by bits of shattered rock.

In November 1943 Nimitz's island-hopping campaign began with his assaults on Betio in the Tarawa Atoll and at Makin a hundred miles north. It was a costly beginning. Elements of the Army's 27th Infantry Division secured Makin with relative ease, but at Betio the 2d Marine Division encountered stubborn and deadly resistance. Naval gunfire and air attacks had failed to eliminate the deeply dug-in defenders, and landing craft grounded on reefs offshore, where they were destroyed by Japanese artillery. As costly as it was, the lessons learned there proved useful in future amphibious operations. Like MacArthur, Nimitz determined to bypass strongly held islands and strike at the enemy's weak points.

During January 1944 landings were made in the Marshalls at Kwajalein and Eniwetok followed by Guam and Saipan in the Marianas during June and July. Because the Marianas were only 1,500 miles from Tokyo, the remaining Japanese carriers came out to fight. The resulting Battle of the Philippine Sea was a disaster for the Japanese. In what U.S. Navy pilots called "the great Marianas turkey shoot," Japanese carrier power was effectively eliminated.

Almost as soon as the Marianas were cleared, the air forces began to prepare airfields to receive new heavy bombers, the B–29s. With a range exceeding 3,000 miles, B–29s could reach most Japanese cities, including Tokyo. In November 1944 the Twentieth Air Force began a strategic bombing campaign against Japan, which indirectly led to one of the bitterest island fights of the war. Tiny Iwo Jima, lying 750 miles southeast of Tokyo, was needed both as an auxiliary base for crippled B–29s returning from their bombing raids over Japan and as a base for long-range escort fighters. The fight for the five-mile-long island lasted five weeks, during February and March 1945, and cost more than 25,000 dead—almost 6,000 Americans of the 4th and 5th Marine Divisions and 20,000 Japanese.

While Nimitz crossed the central Pacific, MacArthur pushed along the New Guinea coast, preparing for his return to the Philippines. Without carriers, his progress was slower but less costly than Nimitz's. After clearing the Buna area in January 1943, MacArthur spent the next year conquering northeastern New Guinea and the eight months that followed moving across the northern coast of Netherlands New Guinea to the island of Morotai. Because he had to cover his landings with land-based planes, he was limited to bounds of 200 miles or less on a line of advance almost 2,000 miles long. Furthermore, he had to build airfields as he went. By October 1944 MacArthur was ready for a leap to the Philippines, but this objective was beyond the range of his planes. Nimitz loaned him Admiral William F. Halsey's heavy car-

*"All Aboard for Home" by Joseph Hirsch. Despite wartime increases, Allied sealift capability remained inadequate to return Army forces home as fast as they would have liked. (*Army Art Collection)

riers, and, on 20 October 1944, MacArthur's Sixth Army landed on Leyte Island in the central Philippines.

The Japanese reacted vigorously. For the first time in the war they employed Kamikaze attacks, suicide missions flown by young, half-trained pilots. And they used their last carriers as decoys to draw Halsey's carriers away from the beachheads. With Halsey out of the battle and the landing forces without air cover, the Japanese planned to use conventional warships to brush aside the remaining American warships and destroy the support vessels anchored off the beaches. They almost succeeded. In the naval Battle of Leyte Gulf, the big guns of the big ships, not carrier planes, decided the battle. The Japanese naval forces were decimated. Japan no longer had an effective navy.

As violent as they were, most island fights involved small units and were mercifully short. However, the last two major campaigns of the Pacific war—Luzon and Okinawa—took on some of the character of the war in Europe. They were long fights on larger land masses, with entire armies in sustained combat over the course of several months. Japanese defenders on Luzon numbered 262,000 under Lt. Gen. Tomoyuki Yamashita, perhaps the best field commander in the *Japanese Army*. Yamashita refused an open battle, knowing that superior firepower and command of the air would favor the Americans. Instead, he prepared defensive positions where his forces could deny the Americans strategic points like roads and airfields. He wanted to force the Americans to attack Japanese positions in a new battle of attrition.

His plan worked. MacArthur's Sixth Army under Lt. Gen. Walter Krueger landed on Luzon on 9 January 1945 and began the Army's longest land campaign in the Pacific. MacArthur's forces fought for almost seven months and took nearly 40,000 casualties before finally subduing the Japanese.

The largest landings of Nimitz's central Pacific drive were carried out on Okinawa, only 300 miles from Japan, on 1 April 1945. Before the fight was over three months later, the entire Tenth Field Army—four Army infantry divisions and two Marine divisions—had been deployed there. Like his counterpart on Luzon, the Japanese commander on Okinawa, Lt. Gen. Mitsuru Ushijima, refused to fight on the beaches and instead withdrew into the rocky hills to force a battle of attrition. Again the strategy worked. U.S. casualties were staggering, the largest of the Pacific war. Over 12,000 American soldiers, sailors, and marines died during the struggle. At Okinawa the Japanese launched the greatest Kamikaze raids of the war, and the results were frightening—26 ships sunk and 168 damaged. Almost 40 percent of the American dead were sailors lost to Kamikaze attacks.

When the Luzon and Okinawa battles ended in July, the invasion of the southernmost Japanese island of Kyushu had already been ordered by the Joint Chiefs. The date was set for 1 November 1945. Kyushu would furnish air and naval bases to intensify the air bombardment and strengthen the naval blockade around Honshu, the main island of Japan. A massive invasion in the Tokyo area was scheduled for 1 March 1946 if Japanese resistance continued. With the Okinawa experience fresh in their minds, many planners feared that the invasion of Japan would produce a bloodbath.

In fact, Japan was already beaten. It was defenseless on the seas; its air force was gone; and its cities were being burned out by incendiary bombs. The atomic bombings of Hiroshima and Nagasaki on 6 and 9 August and the Soviet declaration of war on 8 August forced the leaders of Japan to recognize the inevitable. On 15 August 1945, Emperor Hirohito announced Japan's surrender to the Japanese people and ordered Japanese forces to lay down their arms. Despite their earlier suicidal resistance, they immediately did so. With V-J Day—2 September 1945—the greatest war in human history came to an end.

Aftermath

The United States emerged from the war with global military commitments that included the occupation of Germany and Japan and the oversight of Allied interests in liberated areas. Almost 13 million Americans were in uniform at the end of the war; over 8 million of them were soldiers. But the impulse was strong to follow the patterns of the past and dismantle this force. Families pressed the government to "bring the boys home," and soldiers overseas demanded the acceleration of the separation process. American monopoly of the atomic bomb seemed to furnish all the power that American security interests needed. Some air power advocates even argued that the bomb made armies and navies obsolete.

President Roosevelt had died in April 1945, on the eve of victory. The new President, Harry S. Truman, and his advisers tried to resist the political pressures for hasty demobilization. Truman wanted to retain a postwar Army of 1.5 million, a Navy of 600,000, and an Air Force of 400,000. But neither Congress nor the American public was willing to sustain such a force. Within five months of V-J Day, 8.5 million servicemen and women had been mustered out, and in June of the following year only two full Army divisions were available for deployment in an emergency. By 1947 the Army numbered a mere 700,000—sixth in size among the armies of the world.

Yet too much had changed for the Army to return to its small and insular prewar status. Millions of veterans now remembered their service with pride. The beginning of the Cold War, especially the Berlin blockade of 1948, dramatically emphasized the need to remain strong. The Army had become too deeply intertwined with American life and security to be reduced again to a constabulary force. Moreover, the time was not far off when new conflicts would demonstrate the limits of atomic power and prove that ground forces were as necessary as they had been in the past.

Further Readings

Despite its age, Charles B. MacDonald's *The Mighty Endeavor: American Armed Forces in the European Theater in World War II* (1969) remains a sound, informative, and highly readable survey of the American role in the war in Europe. For the interwar Army, I. B. Holley, jr.'s *General John M. Palmer, Citizen Soldiers and the Army of a Democracy* (1982) is good for the early years. Palmer was the architect of the National Defense Act of 1920. D. Clayton James' *The Years of MacArthur: Volume 1, 1880–1941* (1970), looks at the interwar Army in terms of the man who dominated it in the 1930s, while Forrest Pogue's *George C. Marshall, Volume 1: Education of a General, 1880–1939* (1963), focuses on the man who oversaw its transformation into a powerful, modern mass army. Volume 2: *Ordeal and Hope, 1939–1945* (1986), and Volume 3: *Organizer of Victory, 1943–1945* (1973), are the best sources on the War Department and the General Staff and cover an enormous range of topics from strategy and logistics to personalities.

Len Deighton's *Blitzkrieg: From the Rise of Hitler to the Fall of Dunkirk* (1980) is a popular, semijournalistic account that places German tactical and operational innovations in the context of interwar *German Army* politics and the Nazi rise to power and also discusses the relationship between tactics, equipment, and organization in a nontechnical way. *Fire-Power: British Army Weapons and Theories of War, 1904–1945* (1982), by Shelford Bidwell and Dominick Graham, is a seminal and important book, tracing changes in military doctrine from the perspective of the artillery arm from World War I through World War II. Bidwell and Graham analyze the origins of *Blitzkrieg* tactics and *panzer* organizations and the evolution of indirect artillery fire and their impact on war.

W. G. F. Jackson's *Battle for North Africa, 1940–1943* (1975), is reliable, and Martin Blumenson's *Kasserine Pass* (1967) can be supplemented by Ralph Ingersoll's *The Battle Is the Pay-off* (1943). Written in the immediate aftermath of the Kasserine Pass debacle by a journalist-captain who accompanied the Rangers on their raid against the Italian-held pass at El Guettar, it has the gritty immediacy of a contemporary first-person account and ends with an impassioned plea for tougher physical conditioning and more realistic training.

A useful antidote to grand theoretical speculations about the nature of war is John Ellis' *The Sharp End: The Fighting Man in World War II* (1980). Using a vast array of first-person accounts, Ellis focuses on the experience of frontline combat in both theaters. Ellis has also written *Cassino: Hollow Victory* (1984), a gripping and critical account of Allied attempts to break through the mountains of central Italy, an effort which, the author believes, was crippled by a self-serving and inept Allied high command. Useful companions are Wyford Vaughan-Thomas' *Anzio* (1961) and Martin Blumenson's *Anzio: The Gamble That Failed* (1963).

Max Hastings' *Overlord: D-Day and the Battle for Normandy* (1984) is among the best of the new books on the invasion. A careful and skilled journalist, Hastings asks why it took so long for the Allies to break out of the beachhead. He finds the flawed performance of the citizen armies of Britain and the United States at fault, when compared to the skill and proficiency of the Germans. Russell F. Weigley, in *Eisenhower's Lieutenants: The Campaign of France and Germany, 1944–1945* (1986), asks similar questions about American combat performance and advances a provocative thesis, suggesting that the U.S. Army never reconciled its two conflicting heritages—that of the frontier constabulary, with its emphasis on mobility, and that of U. S. Grant's direct power drive in the Civil War. Thus, U.S. combat formations in World War II were structured for mobility, while American strategy and operations called for head-on confrontations with the center of enemy strength.

Ralph F. Bennett's *ULTRA in the West: The Normandy Campaign, 1944–1945* (1980), heavily based on the original, declassified decrypts, is sound on ULTRA's impact on the land campaign. Charles B. MacDonald's *A Time for Trumpets: The Untold Story of the Battle of the Bulge* (1985) updates earlier accounts of the German Ardennes offensive with the latest available information about the Allied intelligence failure, while his *Company Commander* (1978) is still one of the most moving and honest first-person accounts of small-unit command responsibility available. (MacDonald was one of the youngest captains in the Army in 1944 when his company was hit and overrun in the first hours of the German offensive.)

Stephen Ambrose's *Supreme Commander: The War Years of General Dwight D. Eisenhower* (1970) is a judicious and balanced assessment of Eisenhower from his arrival in Washington in December 1941 through the German surrender in May 1945. Omar N. Bradley's and Clay Blair's *A General's Life* (1983) is a far more partisan biography of the so-called G.I. General, which provides a sometimes disconcerting glimpse of the internal tensions and disagreements within the Allied high command in Europe. It should be balanced with Nigel Hamilton's exhaustive, but also pugnaciously partisan three-volume biography, *Monty: The Making of a General, 1887–1942* (1981), *Monty: Master of the Battlefield, 1942–1944* (1983), and *Monty: Final Years of the Field-Marshal, 1944–1976* (1987), and all can be supplemented by the fairly reliable official histories produced by the American and British military services in the postwar period.

Two general histories provide excellent surveys of the Pacific war, from the causes to the conclusion. John Toland's *The Rising Sun, 1936–1945* (1971), views the war from the Japanese perspective and focuses on the war's causes, Japanese war plans, and the early victorious campaigns from the vantage point of Japan's military leadership. A counterpart volume is *Eagle Against the Sun* (1985) by Ronald H. Spector. Like Toland, Spector covers the entire conflict but views the war from the American perspective. *Eagle Against the Sun* may be the best single-volume survey of the Pacific war yet written.

The historical literature on Pearl Harbor and the first six months of the war in the Pacific is voluminous—so vast that readers must be especially careful in their selections. Perhaps the best picture of life in the prewar army is found in James Jones' fictional *From Here to Eternity* (1985). The subject of Pearl Harbor has produced countless pages of description and analysis, but much is of interest only to professional historians and specialists in the subject. Two books of special value to the general reader are Walter Lord's *Day of Infamy* (1957) and Gordon Prange's *At Dawn We Slept* (1982). *Day of Infamy* begins in the predawn hours and details the fascinating, dramatic events of the day the Japanese attacked Pearl Harbor. The book is short, and Lord writes in a clear, journalistic style. *At Dawn We Slept* is a more complete and exhaustive book on the attack, the events leading to it, and the surrounding controversies. Although the book is over 700 pages long, the style is readable, the story interesting, and the treatment complete. If a student can read only one book on Pearl Harbor, Prange's work is the logical choice.

The best single-volume survey of the first six months in the Pacific after Pearl Harbor is John Toland's *But Not in Shame* (1961), which relates the story of defeat in the Pacific with a true sense of heroism and tragedy. Included are the American defeats at Pearl Harbor, Bataan, Corregidor, and Wake Island, and the Allied failures in the Dutch East Indies and Singapore. Stanley Falk's *Bataan:*

March of Death (1984) is a moving and unbiased account of one of the most emotional subjects in American military history. The battles for Guadalcanal and for Buna went on simultaneously, but Guadalcanal received far more attention from the American press at the time and from historians since that date. However, the quality of the works on Guadalcanal varies greatly. An older but reliable account is *The Battle for Guadalcanal* (1979) by Samuel B. Griffith II, which can be supplemented by Richard Tregaskis' *Guadalcanal Diary* (1984), a classic in war reporting that came out of the fighting on Guadalcanal. For the Papua Campaign, Lida Mayo's *Bloody Buna* (1979) not only chronicles the battles but also effectively conveys the nightmarish qualities of fighting in New Guinea—the constant rain, the disease, the lack of proper food and equipment, and the constant threat of death from the Japanese or from the jungle.

Hundreds, if not thousands, of books have been written on the campaigns that produced victory over Japan in the Pacific war. They range from very detailed volumes in the official histories of the United States Army, Navy, and Marine Corps to highly romanticized books on specific actions, people, weapons, and so forth. The following three books are accurate, balanced, and interesting accounts of the subject. Two sound works covering the offensive period are D. Clayton James' *The Years of MacArthur, 1941–1945* (1975), for the offensives in the Southwest Pacific and the Philippines, and James and William Belote's *Titans of the Seas* (1974), an account of the carrier battles in the Pacific. But no work better describes combat in the Pacific war at the squad and platoon level than *Island Victory* (1983) by S. L. A. Marshall. During World War II as a combat historian he gathered material for *Island Victory* by interviewing infantrymen of the 7th Infantry Division who had just cleared two small islands in the Kwajalein Atoll. The book tells the stories of squad and platoon fights with holed-up Japanese on islands no more than 250 yards wide. There are no generals or colonels here, no high-level planning or strategy. This is the story of ground combat from the vantage point of the individual infantryman, and, like MacDonald's *Company Commander*, the work is a testimony to the determination and heroism of the individual GI.

Note: The publication dates are shown for the most recent editions listed in *Books in Print*. Many of these books were originally published years earlier.